I WAN ... HAIR

I WANT THAT HAIR

by Jane Thornton

JOSEF WEINBERGER PLAYS

LONDON

I WANT THAT HAIR
First published in 2007
by Josef Weinberger Ltd
12-14 Mortimer Street, London, W1T 3JJ
www.josef-weinberger.com
general.info@jwmail.co.uk

ISBN   978 0 85676 297 0 (13 digit)
         0 85676 297 0 (10 digit)

Printed in England by Commercial Colour Press plc, Hainault, Essex

I WANT THAT HAIR was first produced by Hull Truck Theatre
(John Godber, Artistic Director) at the Hull Truck Theatre,
Spring Street, Hull, on 2 February 2006 prior to a national UK
tour. The cast was as follows:

BEX	Gillian Jephcott
HEIDI	Kiki Kendrick

Directed by John Godber

Designed by Pip Leckenby

Lighting Designed by Graham Kirk

ACT ONE

Scene One

A realistic hair salon, somewhere in Yorkshire. It is modern but was last updated some ten years ago and as a result is now worn around the edges: greying paintwork, well worn black leather chairs. The audience are the main mirrors but there are small shelves at knee height on which to place equipment such as hairdryers and a radio. There is a need for working plugs. There is an entrance up stage right and a storeroom off stage left. Up stage left there are two sinks. Around the salon are trolleys with hairdressing equipment, a hairdryer on wheels, towel storage and shelves full of products and free gifts. There is a desk near the door with a phone and appointment book.

Lights.

Bex *is about to turn forty. She is smartly dressed, trendy but practical.* Heidi *is forty-two, more mutton dressed as lamb. She has streaked hair, a false tan and a good figure supported by high shoes.* Bex *is blow drying a* Client's *hair (a stage-management role which is non-speaking and required in three scenes only).* Bex *speaks over the sound of the hairdryer and the radio, which is playing loudly in the background.*

BEX   I mean that's the thing about Max, he's always wanting to change things. We should double our mortgage and get somewhere bigger he says! Never satisfied; he's on about getting one of these hot tubs now, but I've got no idea where he's going to put it!

               (*Calls off.*)

               India! I think that's why he wants to flit, just to get a hot tub! India! Where is she?

               (*Phone rings.* Heidi *enters carrying the salon's portable phone.*)

HEIDI   She went for a sandwich an hour ago!

BEX	Where to?
HEIDI	I didn't ask her!

(HEIDI *answers the phone.*)

HEIDI	"I Want That Hair!" No, it's "I Want That Hair", why, who are you looking for love?

(HEIDI *has exited with the phone.*)

BEX	Mind you as soon as we'd moved in he wanted to move out again, thought that we'd under invested. I think he expects me to be in here when I'm sixty.

(*calls off*) India!

I mean my mother was but . . . (*Calls off.*) Is there another coffee?

(HEIDI *re-enters on the phone.*)

HEIDI	No this is "I Want That Hair", "Hairsperience" is six, four, five, this is six, three, five. It's just across the road. What do you mean can I go across and make a booking for you, can I hell! (HEIDI *exits as she calls.*) Cheeky gett!
BEX	(*shouts*) India? Mind you my mother worked herself into the ground in here. I think Max expects me to do the same. He's bloody had that, I've told him he's the breadwinner, he's got the big ideas! Just because he lives for work I think he expects me to do the same! And I mean our Rachel's fourteen now, and what she doesn't want! Mind you we could do with flitting because you can't swing a cat in her bedroom to be honest.

(HEIDI *enters with the phone.*)

HEIDI	Do we want to change our phone supplier?

BEX	Get their home number and tell 'em we'll call 'em back! (*Back to* CLIENT.) No, I don't know what to do!
HEIDI	(*to the phone*) I'll tell you what give us your home number and we'll call you at home love! (*To* BEX.) He says he can't give us his home number!
BEX	Well tell him not to call us at home then!
HEIDI	We're not at home though are we?
BEX	He doesn't bloody know that does he?
HEIDI	No he doesn't does he!
BEX	I mean my mother used to live above the shop didn't she?
	(HEIDI *looks at* BEX *and then the phone. She speaks down the phone.*)
HEIDI	Listen don't call us at home; and don't call again or we'll tell the police you're stalking us. Yes I know it's a recorded call so stick it up your arse mate! (*To* BEX.) He's gone!
	(*Music. Blackout.*)

Scene Two

HEIDI *is chewing whilst talking* BEX *is listening as she dries her* CLIENT'*s hair.*

HEIDI	Anyway Becky I says to her, "Trinity, I can't. Don't be daft, I can't. How can I?" And she says, "'course you can" and I says, "I can't". So she says, "why can't you?" And I says, "I don't want to" and she says, "why don't you? You don't know what you're missing" and I think, I hardly know you! So I says, "to be honest it's not my sort of thing". So she says,

well you don't know until you've tried it". And
I says, "Trinity, I do" and she says, "no you
don't. It changed my life". And I thought well
it needed chuffin' changing didn't it? She's
thirty-seven and she still lives with her mam
and dad in a static caravan. Then she says
she'll lend me the money! I couldn't believe it!

BEX   She's got no friends, that's why!

HEIDI   Why me though? Have I got "sad bastard"
             tattooed on my head or sommat?

BEX   Not yet!

HEIDI   Because I'll tell you sommat, I don't need the
             money and I don't need to go to chuffin'
             Gambia to get a bloke, I've got one. And if I
             wanted another I could get one down t'
             Gardener's Arms. Mind you most of 'em have
             got two heads down there and are brickies but
             . . . Mind you if you go in the Brickie's Arms
             for a drink it's full of plumbers so you just
             never where you are . . .

             (*The* CLIENT *winces.*)

BEX   We need a plumber to fix that shower so that
             could be handy! Sorry, did I burn you?

             (*The phone rings.* HEIDI *takes the call.*)

HEIDI   Hello, "I Want that Hair!" No I've got the hair
             mate! Oh it's him again from the telephone!
             Listen I've told you once you soft gett! Get off
             the line there's train coming!

BEX   (*to* CLIENT) Now you can see why I have Heidi,
             it's because she's got such a good telephone
             manner!

HEIDI   Oh sod 'em, that's what I think!

(*Music. Blackout.*)

Scene Three

BEX *is on the phone and is looking in the appointment book.*
HEIDI *is removing the cape and towels, etc, from the* CLIENT.

BEX	Not Tuesday. No. Nothing sorry.
HEIDI	(*to* CLIENT) Did you have a coat?
BEX	It would have to be me on Tuesday . . .

(HEIDI'S *mobile phone rings. She picks it up.*)

HEIDI	(*to* CLIENT) Won't be a minute. (*To phone.*) Hiya.
BEX	Heidi! Can you do Mrs McGlynn on Tuesday after those extensions?
HEIDI	(*to phone*) No, it's not gone to my chest.
BEX	Can you fit Mrs McGlynn in?
HEIDI	(*to phone*) I know but you should see what I'm coughing up though (*To* CLIENT.) Is it the black one? (*To phone.*) No, I'm still at work, where do you think I am? I can't just be there when you want me, mam.

(HEIDI *unhooks a black coat from upstage.*)

BEX	(*inspecting the book*) Tuesday's ever so busy!
HEIDI	(*to phone*) He's never . . .
BEX	That's my coat, by the way.
HEIDI	(*holding coat*) What this, is it new? It's nice is that! Did Max buy it you? What is it, an early birthday present?

BEX   How long will them extensions take on
            Tuesday?

HEIDI   Two hours, maybe three. (*To phone.*) Well tell
            him you want that one from the Argos. (*To*
            CLIENT.) It's the pink one, isn't it?

BEX   So you've no space?

HEIDI   (*nods her head, to phone*) That Elizabeth Duke,
            no it'll be lovely that.

            (HEIDI *helping to put* CLIENT's *coat on.*)

BEX   Well what about Wednesday?

HEIDI   Well it's about time he spent sommat, isn't it?
            Well I can't do owt about that, Mam; it's his
            dog, isn't it? He should wash it!

            (BEX *looks at the appointment book and
            speaks into the phone.*)

BEX   I think I might be able to squeeze you in on
            Thursday morning before the plumbers visit
            and the dog's wash and blow dry, is that any
            good for you?

            (*Music.*)

            (HEIDI *helps the* CLIENT *into her coat, looks at
            her, puts her hood up for her and sends her on
            her way.*)

            (*Blackout.*)

                          Scene Four

Later; much quieter. BEX *sits. She takes her shoe off and
slowly inspects her foot.*

BEX   Look at that! Bloody Hell!

            (*Enter* HEIDI *carrying towels which she starts
            to fold and put away.*)

Is that a carbuncle? I'm getting a carbuncle, aren't I?

(HEIDI *inspects* BEX'S *foot.*)

HEIDI   I can't see owt.

BEX   Are you looking?

HEIDI   'Course I'm looking.

BEX   Can't you see a carbuncle?

HEIDI   What do they look like?

BEX   They look like a bloody carbuncle!

HEIDI   No, I can't see owt. It just looks a like a bit of hard skin that's swollen.

BEX   That'll be my carbuncle then!

HEIDI   (*grimaces*) Oh yes! Awful, that carbuncle!

BEX   That's with me being stood up all these years. Can you believe it? I'm not even forty and I've got my mother's bloody feet!

HEIDI   You are tomorra!

(*Music. Blackout.*)

Scene Five

BEX *and* HEIDI *sit.* HEIDI *flicks through a magazine.* BEX *is rubbing her feet with some cream.*

HEIDI   Ten hours today, there's no wonder you've got bad feet.

BEX   I think I'm going to have to get some Scholl's or something.

HEIDI	I'd rather be crippled than wear Scholl's. You know who wears Scholl's, don't you?
BEX	Who?
HEIDI	What they call her . . . Mrs Whatsit! Vicar's thingy!
BEX	Mrs Vicary?
HEIDI	Eh?
BEX	Who?
HEIDI	Her who does the Vicar's thingy, cleaning! Mrs Whatsit!
BEX	Mrs Whitham?
HEIDI	She wears 'em.
BEX	Mrs Whitham? Does she?
HEIDI	Mind you, she's got fat feet, hasn't she? She probably can't get owt else on!
BEX	That's her heart that!
HEIDI	She smells and all, doesn't she?
BEX	Well that's her hormones that, isn't it?
HEIDI	I mean I feel a bit sorry for her, but I hate doing her hair. She's got that many complaints you never know if you're going to catch owt.
BEX	Well it's her age, isn't it?
HEIDI	She needs hosing down.
BEX	She can't help that, that's just how she is! She's got personal problems, hasn't she?
HEIDI	Well if you feel so sympathetic towards her why do you allus give her to me?

BEX   I didn't say she didn't smell, I just said it's her hormones, her heart and her age! I mean she stinks to high heaven but it's just how she is, isn't it?

    (*A beat.*)

HEIDI I'll start to get done then!

    (HEIDI *tidies up.*)

BEX   What have we had today, can you remember?

HEIDI (*from off*) Two perms. Three colours. Some highlights. Two blokes. Four cut and blow-drys. That kid with nits.

BEX   Did you see the size of them?

HEIDI And your Gloria!

BEX   She's not my Gloria.

HEIDI She's your mother-in-law.

BEX   What was she after anyway?

HEIDI Oh you know Gloria! And a bridal practice. Looked really nice that, didn't it?

BEX   She didn't like it though, did she?

HEIDI Didn't she?

BEX   She said that she wants it up.

HEIDI Up?

BEX   She nearly had it up, but not on top of her head.

HEIDI She's had her tits done her, you know.

BEX   Who?

HEIDI   Her!

BEX   Has she?

HEIDI   She's had her tits done!

BEX   What, bigger or smaller?

HEIDI   Bigger.

BEX   You can't really tell though, can you?

HEIDI   You should have seen her before, she only had
         fried eggs.

BEX   Fried eggs?

HEIDI   Well, you know!

BEX   You do come out with some stuff!

HEIDI   Well she has, because she told me. Her dad
         paid for it apparently, for a wedding present.

BEX   You're joking?

HEIDI   I'm not.

BEX   Her having her tits done was on her wedding
         list?

HEIDI   I'm not saying that, but I know that he paid for
         her to have 'em done because she told our
         Lucy in Argos!

BEX   She gets about then!

HEIDI   Mind you she's had some problems with 'em;
         you know that she works in Morrisons?

BEX   Who, your Lucy?

HEIDI   No her! Haven't you seen her on the checkout?

BEX   I don't go to Morrisons!

HEIDI   Well you should because it's a lot cheaper,
               you know!

BEX   No I don't like Morrisons!

HEIDI   There's more reasons to shop at Morrisons!

BEX   I go to Sainsbury's mostly, but it's ever so
               expensive.

HEIDI   You should try Morrisons.

BEX   Yes they say it's a lot cheaper, don't they?

HEIDI   Well anyway, I don't know whether it's
               because she went back to work early after the
               operation or what, but obviously she's having
               to move her arm a lot and one of them starts
               leaking.

BEX   What, one of her arms?

HEIDI   She had to go back and get it fixed.

BEX   Not to Kwik-Fit?

HEIDI   I don't know where she went, but it was leaking
               all over apparently!

BEX   It might have gone all over somebody's
               shopping.

               (*A beat.*)

HEIDI   To be honest I'd have mine done if I could
               afford it.

BEX   Stick it on your wedding list then.

HEIDI   Oh listen, once bitten, twice shy!

               (*A beat.*)

BEX	No, I'm too squeamish and like you say too many things can go wrong.
HEIDI	I mean I don't want to be like Jordan or owt but I wouldn't mind being more pert.
BEX	Have you noticed as you get older that all your stuffing starts moving downwards. I mean the the thing is, if you did have it done where would you stop? You have your tits done then you think, "my legs look shit", then it's your nose and then what?
HEIDI	You'd look like Anne Robinson.

(*A beat.*)

Right we'll get off then, shall we?

BEX	What about the floor?
HEIDI	Well I thought seeing as we've got a party to go to . . .
BEX	(*assertive*) No, I want it doing now!
HEIDI	Well we could do it tomorra morning.
BEX	(*unhinged*) No, I said I want it doing now alright!

(*Silence.*)

HEIDI	Well I'd better do it now then!

(HEIDI *plugs in a hairdryer and starts blowing out the hair from under the pipes and the chairs, etc.*)

BEX	I want it to be all left clean.
HEIDI	Can't hear you.
BEX	And these trolleys are full of stuff as well.

HEIDI   Eh?

BEX   (*shouts*) These trolleys, want sorting.

HEIDI   (*turns off hairdryer*) India was supposed to do
               that.

BEX   Where is she?

HEIDI   She went out for a sandwich!

BEX   Did you say she could?

HEIDI   I said she could go for a sandwich, I didn't tell
               her to be lost in action! But you might as well
               talk to the wall . . .

               (BEX *gets a brush and starts to sweep.*)

BEX   Bloody India? Where did they get that from? I
               bet that family has never been to Torquay.

               (*A beat.*)

HEIDI   Mind you, I haven't.

BEX   What, Torquay?

HEIDI   I've never been, I've only ever been to one
               place on the south coast and that was Tenby.

BEX   Tenby isn't on the south coast.

HEIDI   That's the only place I've ever been down
               there; that and Newquay!

BEX   You know I bet her family haven't been out of
               the country, and they christened her India!

HEIDI   Wishful thinking maybe!

BEX   I mean I've met her dad, he's lucky if he gets
               out of the bloody chair.

HEIDI	I think it's a nice name: India, conjures up a picture of someone exotic!
BEX	Yes but she's about as exotic as a tin of soup.
HEIDI	Mind you, you can get exotic soup now though.
BEX	Not in tins you can't.
HEIDI	Yes you can!
BEX	Exotic soup is always in cartons.

(*A beat.*)

HEIDI	I'll go get the mop.
BEX	And make sure you squirt some of that disinfectant stuff in.
HEIDI	(*as she exits*) Hey, I know how to mop a chuffin' floor.
BEX	(*calls off*) She took the hair straighteners home last week, the ceramic ones, didn't even ask. The trouble was she got caught out; forgot to bring them back. I had to send her home in a taxi to get them, I took that out of her wage.
HEIDI	(*from off*) I bet she loves you.
BEX	I don't care. I'm not having it from her.

(HEIDI *appears with a mop and bucket.*)

HEIDI	(*mopping*) To be honest they're all the same, aren't they? None of them has any idea. They don't even think to sweep up unless you tell 'em. They're allergic to hard work.
BEX	We weren't like that, were we?

HEIDI   (*mopping*) Well I was! When I was training, I'd
          be late back from my dinner and say that I'd
          lost my purse. I'd been shopping like, I just
          couldn't stand going back. I was a brilliant liar
          then, all teenagers are. Maybe they should be
          able to sit an exam in it. "Come in, sit down,
          now your first question is, have you ever been
          to the pub?" "A Pub? No. I'm not old enough
          am I? I've just been around to my mates."
          "Well done two points." "Question two, have
          you ever slept with your boyfriend?" "Who
          me? 'Course not, I'm saving it until I get
          married!"

BEX   Rachael's starting with all that.

HEIDI   Lying or boyfriends?

BEX   You put all that into 'em and then suddenly all
          you get back is a grunt.

HEIDI   Eh?

          (BEX *watching* HEIDI.)

          Make sure you do that corner, it never gets
          done, that!

          (HEIDI *stops and looks at* BEX.)

HEIDI   This corner? I always do this corner! It's you
          that never does it!

          (HEIDI *mops on.*)

BEX   I look at her and I think where's that little girl
          who had rainbow trousers gone?

HEIDI   Mind you I had rainbow trousers once.

BEX   Yes but you were thirty-eight, darling!

HEIDI   (*mopping*) It's filthy, this corner!

BEX	Where's that little hand I used to hold?
HEIDI	(*mopping*) It goes too quick. I realised that with our Dean!
BEX	I thought you only had Lucy?
HEIDI	No, I had our Dean first, I was only as old as India.
BEX	I thought you just had one like me! I thought that was at least something we had in common.
HEIDI	No I had our Dean first.
BEX	See, that's something else that I didn't know about you!
HEIDI	(*still sweeping*) Oh aye, I'm all secrets me!

(BEX *takes a deep breath and starts sorting out the trollies*.)

BEX	Anyway Monday I'll ring the college and tell them that exotic India needs to buck up her ideas.
HEIDI	If they ever find her!
BEX	Oh, when was this last done?
HEIDI	You don't have to have been somewhere in order to name your kid after it anyway, you know?
BEX	I know, but how did you get stuck with Heidi?
HEIDI	My dad was in the army.
BEX	There you go then!
HEIDI	I mean I look in the mirror even now and I think; I'm not an Heidi. Heidis carry milk about

and play with goats! And they speak German. I mean I don't speak bloody German. I can only just speak English! And look at our Lucy's little 'un, she's called her Savannah and she's never even been to Africa!

BEX Well there you go then!

HEIDI I think she just likes elephants, that's all!

BEX (*still cleaning*) That'll be it then.

(HEIDI *has completed her mopping.*)

HEIDI Right! All done, try not to walk on it.

(BEX *looks at the floor.*)

BEX It never comes up good any more. In fact the whole place needs a face-lift especially now they've opened that across 'road.

HEIDI They've done it up nice, haven't they?

BEX I don't know, I've not been in!

HEIDI Yes it's all sort of browns and creams.

BEX Is it sort of browns and creams, or is it browns and creams?

HEIDI It's browns and creams!

BEX As long as we know!

HEIDI It's all modern.

BEX They had brown and cream in 1975.

HEIDI They do everything you know, all the beauty stuff.

BEX   Nobody wants it though do they, it's a faceless
             experience; it'll be closed in a couple of
             months!

HEIDI   Well they reckon they've got six months worth
             of bookings already, it was in the paper, the
             bloke who owns it is on about opening another
             one in Goole or somewhere!

BEX   Goole?

HEIDI   Or somewhere.

BEX   Goole . . . hell, whatever next?

HEIDI   Goole or somewhere!

BEX   So it might not be Goole?

HEIDI   It's Goole or somewhere.

BEX   Max went to school in Goole. Goole Grammar
             School.

HEIDI   They're going to be all over the north.

             (*A beat.*)

BEX   Well we haven't got room to develop here,
             have we?

             (HEIDI *walks towards the fourth wall and
             looks across the road*.)

HEIDI   Shit name though, "Hairsperience". What's it
             mean do you think?

BEX   I've no idea! But that's not the point!

HEIDI   One of them has got pink hair. Have you seen
             him?

BEX   He doesn't go with the browns and creams
             though, does he?

HEIDI	He's got pink hair, and a stud and all!
BEX	I had pink hair once you know? Can you believe it? Pink hair and Doc Martens shoes! And now look at me. Mrs Marks and Spencer's catalogue! You don't fancy having a cuppa do you? I haven't had my daily intake! India was supposed to be sorting that before she left us for a better place!
HEIDI	You haven't got time though, have you? You need to go home and get ready for your surprise party.
BEX	It's not much of a surprise though, is it. I've known all about it for two months!
HEIDI	Well I've got to get ready, I want to look smart.
BEX	What to surprise me?
HEIDI	You should see what I'm wearing, that'll surprise you.
BEX	Well I hope you're not hanging out of it like you were at Christmas, because Max's dad can't keep his eyes off you as it is! And you know that he's got a bad heart!
HEIDI	It's older men, I can't leave 'em alone!
BEX	Heidi, he's seventy-eight!
HEIDI	Exactly. He should know what it's all about!
	(*Music. Blackout.*)

Scene Six

Ten minutes later. BEX *and* HEIDI *are finishing cups of tea.*
BEX *offers* HEIDI *a biscuit.*

BEX	Don't you want a biscuit?

HEIDI   No, three points.

BEX   Hey?

HEIDI   Three points.

BEX   What is?

HEIDI   Weight Watchers. Three points. I can't have
             one of them if I'm gonna have a drink.

             (*They drink their tea.* BEX *eats a biscuit.*)

BEX   You know we don't really talk much usually, do
             we?

HEIDI   Not to each other, not really.

BEX   I mean it's more like psychiatry than
             hairdressing sometimes, isn't it?

HEIDI   You're not wrong there! You know that Sandra
             whose husband went off with the woman from
             the double glazing firm after her mother had
             died after jumping off the bridge?

BEX   Oh yes her, I know her mother. Well I did.

HEIDI   Well she was telling me that she's out every
             night; desperate to pick somebody up.

BEX   I don't know what it is with you, you rinse their
             hair and it all comes out!

HEIDI   But apparently she's only attracted to blokes
             who've been in trouble and look as rough as
             shit.

BEX   So work that out!

HEIDI   And you know that other one with all the
             money?

BEX   Carlene?

HEIDI	She's not got money!
BEX	She thinks she has!
HEIDI	She thinks she has, but she comes from our estate, her. She's from Birdwell Avenue her, her brother used to pee in our hedges instead of using their loo. I think that's what made my dad bad with his nerves!
BEX	She spends a fortune, though.
HEIDI	When she's got it she does. Her husband's a gambler; met him down the Chinese.
BEX	Which Chinese?
HEIDI	Down the Casino.
BEX	That's not a Chinese.
HEIDI	No but it's full of 'em. Have you noticed how she doesn't come in every week? She only comes in when he's won sommat! If she comes in for short back and sides you know his lucks run out! Anyway I'm not on about her, I mean that Lisa!
BEX	Which Lisa?
HEIDI	Lisa 'My Dad's Won 'Lottery'.
BEX	Oh, Lisa 'My Dad's Won 'Lottery'! I know her.
HEIDI	Well she is loaded her, her dad won the lottery.
BEX	He never?
HEIDI	But she can't keep a bloke.
BEX	She probably can't trust 'em? How much did he win, fifteen million wasn't it?
HEIDI	Well she's had a kid to one of 'em.

BEX	One of who?
HEIDI	One of the blokes, she was only with him a month.
BEX	How do you know?
HEIDI	She told me. I think he was Italian. They tell me everything!
BEX	Well they don't tell me.
HEIDI	They tell me everything, a bit of conditioner on and it all comes out!
BEX	Italian. I mean I know about Mrs Whitham's dog having had pups, but that's as far as it goes with me, I think they think I'm too prissy! I'll tell you what I do know though; Suzy Singer has to have her arms waxed.
HEIDI	Oh that's obvious.
BEX	Why is it?
HEIDI	Because he's a bloke!
BEX	What?
HEIDI	You must have noticed.
BEX	She's never!
HEIDI	Have you seen the size of his hands?
BEX	Is that what you're basing it on?
HEIDI	No, I followed him into the loo and the seat was up!
BEX	Bloody hell, Poirot!

HEIDI	Anyway my Auntie Sheila told me, and her best friend's cousin's daughter is his sister. And the names a give away isn't it? Suzy Singer?
BEX	Singer's Jewish.
HEIDI	Suzy isn't.
BEX	It could be!

(*A beat.*)

HEIDI	So I'd better ring Gary and tell him that I'm going to be late then.
BEX	I thought you were coming on your own.
HEIDI	To a party?
BEX	Well we don't really know Gary, do we?
HEIDI	Well you've met him.
BEX	Once, when he fixed the sink.
HEIDI	I didn't realise the invitation was just for me.
BEX	I was hoping it might just be close friends.

(*A beat.*)

	I mean has he still got a ponytail and all that?
HEIDI	Well he did have this morning. And a pig's arsehole he's had tattooed over his face, it looks nice.
BEX	It's just that Gloria's coming and you know what she's like.
HEIDI	Don't worry, we'll sit in a corner with a bag on our heads!

(*She gathers up the cups and takes them to the storeroom.*)

BEX   So has he moved in then?

HEIDI   (*off*) Not yet! He just stays now and again.

BEX   (*calling off*) No I don't think I could do that, if Max left me; go straight into a new relationship. I think I'd just want to be on my own for a bit.

(HEIDI *re-enters.*)

HEIDI   What and cry yourself senseless? What good would that do? Anyway, it's not exactly the first time it's happened to me is it?

BEX   Well I couldn't let anybody see me naked for a start.

HEIDI   Turn the light off!

(HEIDI *looks to busy herself.*)

So how come Gloria's has been invited then?

BEX   Because Max has organised it. And Rachael says he's asked my dad. So if you see a bloke in a Millets jumper avoid him, he'll bore you to death at fifty yards. He'll either get you on his greenhouse or how many times that day he's had a shit!

HEIDI   So there will be somebody for Gary to talk to then!

BEX   The whole thing is a nightmare to me anyway. I don't want a party, and I certainly don't want a surprise party that I know all about!

HEIDI   Forty's not old you know. I don't feel old and I'm forty two. Anyway life begins at forty.

BEX	Apparently.
HEIDI	In fact, now they're saying that fifty is the new thirty.
BEX	Are they?
HEIDI	Which means that forty is the new twenty.
BEX	That's good then.
HEIDI	Which means that twenty is the new . . .
BEX	Birth, presumably.
HEIDI	Maybe they're saying that fifty is the new forty?
BEX	Maybe forty is forty and it always bloody will be?

(HEIDI *goes to pick some rollers up from in front of the mirror.*)

HEIDI	You need some new rollers this size, there's hardly any left.
BEX	Where have they gone then?
HEIDI	Gone to India I think.

(HEIDI *has been inspecting herself in the mirror.*)

Oh no! Have you seen this? I'm getting a beard. In this light I can see it, there's a load of hairs on my chin.

BEX	Where?
HEIDI	Have we got any tweezers?
BEX	In my bag.

HEIDI	Quick, get me 'em.
	(BEX *goes to get them.*)
	I can't understand why I haven't noticed them before. Did you notice?
BEX	No not really.
HEIDI	Not really, what do you mean, not really?
	(HEIDI *pulls one out with the tweezers.*)
	Look at me I'm turning into a bleedin' leprechaun.
BEX	I thought you said age didn't matter?
HEIDI	I hope to God Gary hasn't noticed.
BEX	Maybe he likes it, maybe it'll turn him on. He's got a ponytail, you've got a beard, it's a matching pair.
HEIDI	Bollocks you, you're not funny. I mean look at me, I'm sprouting! I've got hair coming out all over!
	(HEIDI *stops her hair removal.*)
BEX	You've got one hair, dare to be different!
HEIDI	Why, what would you do, leave it?
BEX	Listen I had a pink Mohican in 1981. I had hairs everywhere then. I've not always been boring! In fact I wish I was more like that now.
HEIDI	So what's stopping you?
BEX	I've got too much to worry about, that's what stopping me!

HEIDI	Like what, you've got a husband, a nice kid, and a big house, at least you're not turning into the bearded woman.
BEX	You know if Max said shall we go to Turkey for a holiday, I'd say no, because I'd be worrying in case we got bird flu.
HEIDI	Well yes . . .
BEX	I mean I'm on a train, and I start worrying that if it crashes, would I survive and who would help me?
HEIDI	Why?
BEX	And if I'm not worrying I'm fantasising.
HEIDI	Well now you're talking!
BEX	It happens when I'm driving mostly. I start to think: "I could just drive to the airport, get on a plane and go to Australia". Or I'm at dinner do with Max and everybody's looking at what I'm wearing and I think: "I might just take my clothes off, see what they'd make of that!"
HEIDI	Oh hell!
BEX	I'll get in the shower.
HEIDI	Well make sure it's a cold one 'coz I think you're going chuffin' crackers! (*To mirror.*) I've got a bloody beard here!

(*Music. Blackout.*)

Scene Seven

HEIDI *is on her mobile, she moves around the salon looking at things and absent-mindedly picking up various objects.*

HEIDI   I don't know how long . . . She's having one of
                   her do's. No I haven't, not yet! Well it's not
                   fair is it, not tonight! I'll ring you back. Yeh
                   that would be good but don't have the iron on
                   too hot. That black one, yeh. Thanks darling,
                   you're a star . . . Have you? What is it? What
                   sort of surprise? . . . Oh you are so mucky, why
                   are you such an animal? No don't, I'm going
                   red . . . Don't, I've got to go . . . All right then
                   . . . 'course I do! I've just said haven't I?

                   (*Music. Blackout.*)

                   Scene Eight

BEX *has a dressing gown on, she has just come out of the*
shower. HEIDI *is applying lipstick.*

HEIDI   I love this colour. Red Alert! I like people to
                   see I've got it on. Gorgeous that!

                   (HEIDI *looks at herself as* BEX *enters.*)

BEX   What did Gloria have to say for herself then?

HEIDI   Well you're not going to like it.

BEX   Why aren't I?

HEIDI   Because she said, it was nowt personal but
                   she's gonna start going over the road.

                   (*A beat.*)

BEX   Why?

HEIDI   Because she can have a proper head massage
                   first.

BEX   Why didn't she tell me then?

HEIDI   Because she's a clucker!

BEX	Yes, a right miserable clucker, if you ask me!
HEIDI	No, a chicken, she was scared to. She thinks she's it with that scarf and her chuffin' wicker basket. Is she posher than the Queen or is it my imagination?
BEX	She only started coming here in the first place because she felt obliged to, she thinks we're down market.
HEIDI	You're gonna have to watch it or they'll all start going across there, won't they?
BEX	No, it's too expensive for a start. I mean do you think Mrs Whitham is going to pay seventy-two quid for a cut and blow dry? She can buy two new pairs of Scholl's with that.
HEIDI	And an all-over body wash.
BEX	Besides, she's a Christian, she can't be seen to be spending all that on her hair, it's immoral. I don't know how they dare charge what they do! I mean it's the same shampoo. There's just a puff in a pink shirt doing a bit of snipping . . .
HEIDI	And he's got pierced nipples!
BEX	How do you know?
HEIDI	People tell me stuff! I've got one of them faces. Come on get on here and I'll start your hair!
	(BEX *moves to a chair so that* HEIDI *can start her hair. She spins her in the chair for a moment.*)
BEX	Anyway I've been thinking, we should have a new image in here, maybe retro or something.
HEIDI	(*combing* BEX's *hair*) Retro? You've got that now, it's that long since you've had it done. If you wait any longer this style will come back

round again! But everybody'll be across the
road having their nipples done.

BEX   Gloria's always been like that anyway!

HEIDI   (*fantasising*) I think you should have it
            Japanese.

BEX   Always been aspiring, my mum hated her. She
            always had to have the latest thing.

HEIDI   (*fantasising*) You could have a water feature
            with some Koi and a big fat Budda sitting
            under a plant . . .

BEX   When I first met Max, she was always having
            parties.

HEIDI   (*joking*) You could shave your head, and dress
            like a monk!

BEX   She thought she was it because she was the
            first in their street to have a marble top
            breakfast bar and she used to put all the drinks
            on it and serve you from it.

HEIDI   (*fabricating*) And you could call it "I Want
            That Zen Hair!"

            (HEIDI *now starts to fashion* BEX'S *hair. She
            may tong it, straighten it or whatever is
            appropriate.*)

BEX   She did them snowballs with little cherries on
            sticks and Babycham in them glasses with a
            deer on that she'd nicked from the
            Conservative Club.

HEIDI   I never been inside that Conservative Club.
            And I've lived round here forty-two years!
            Mind you I've never been in the Labour Club
            either so I suppose that's fair!

BEX   And she always had cheese and pineapple on sticks, and celery and cold curried baked beans to dip it in.

HEIDI   Where the frigging hell did she get that idea from?

BEX   Not from Jamie Oliver.

HEIDI   Cold curried baked beans, she should be locked up.

BEX   And there was no music either, it was just Max's dad playing *Streets of London* and Abba songs on the organ.

           (HEIDI *cannot belive this and stops what she is doing.*)

HEIDI   And that was supposed to be a party?

BEX   Oh yes they knew how to live!

HEIDI   Well I hope he isn't going to play his friggin' organ tonight. I'm at least expecting a dance, and not to *Streets of London*, we'll all be hanging from the ceiling if they play that!

BEX   I can't believe it when I think back!

HEIDI   (*adjusting* BEX) Just sit still will you! So how long have you known Max and the happy family then? Twenty years must be?

BEX   More!

HEIDI   Chuffin' hell!

BEX   Funny thing is I thought it was great. I thought they were posh. I wanted to be like them.

HEIDI   Sounds like they were posher than us.

BEX	Gloria invited my mum and dad once, but when they got there they didn't know what to say.
HEIDI	I should think not, Jesus! Max's dad on his organ singing *Dancing Queen,* what could you say? "Loving me loving you".
BEX	I was embarrassed by them to be honest, I just wanted them to go home.
HEIDI	Do you think they didn't?
BEX	It was like two worlds colliding; I thought my mum and dad were such arseholes for not enjoying it.
HEIDI	Hey listen, they can't have been as bad as my mam and dad. They'd go down to the club; my dad would get pissed up and my mam would bring all the left over pork pies and sausage rolls back in her handbag.
BEX	I thought your dad had been in the army?
HEIDI	He'd been in Dortmund for three weeks training and then he was discharged because of his chest. Then my mam went cleaning and my dad never had a proper job after that. He worked on Parks and Gardens for a bit but my mam said as soon as winter came he packed it in. He did some labouring in the summer and car spraying, then he collected 'pools for a bit.
BEX	My dad did the pools.
HEIDI	Mine sent me 'round to t' neighbours to collect t' money. Everyone of 'em had dogs, except for Mrs Bloomer; She was the only one who didn't smell of cooking fat. She used to give me a cuddle and a Quality Street.
BEX	My dad lived for his work. He was at never at home.

HEIDI	Well that wasn't your fault was it?
BEX	Well it was in a way. I wish now that they could have been more like Max's parents.
HEIDI	What, putting celery dippers in cold curried baked beans and singing, "I hear the drums Fernado?" Chuff me, spare 'em!
BEX	No, able to go to Spain for their holidays and stuff instead of saving to put me through college.
HEIDI	Yes, bit of a waste of time that really when you think about it!
BEX	Well I wouldn't say that!
HEIDI	But you've ended up in the same place as me, haven't you? I've only got three CSEs and I just scraped through Tech. You don't need a degree for hairdressing.
BEX	I thought it would give me a choice.
HEIDI	So why was it that you packed-in teaching then?
	(HEIDI *pulls* BEX'S *hair and she reacts.*)
BEX	For God's sake, steady.
HEIDI	Soz.
BEX	Do you know how to use that?
HEIDI	Yeh.
BEX	You could have fooled me.
HEIDI	You need to get to the roots. By the way, they're showing through.
BEX	They're okay.

HEIDI	They're showing through, though. I can see 'em.
BEX	So, what do you want me to do? Have them done now?
HEIDI	No, I'm just telling you, that's all.
BEX	No wonder Gloria's going across the road.
HEIDI	It's going to look dead good is this.
BEX	Do it softer at the front.
HEIDI	I'm going to. Trust me, it's gonna look cool.
	(*A beat.*)
BEX	What was I saying?
HEIDI	Why you gave up teaching and ran away to the hairdresser's . . .
BEX	It was by default.
HEIDI	Who's fault?
BEX	Default. My mum's . . .
HEIDI	Your mum's fault?
BEX	When she became ill, she needed help or the salon would have had to close.
HEIDI	Was this always your mum's place then?
BEX	She opened in 1964. It was Shirley's then.
HEIDI	(*adjusting her head*) Just look that way.
BEX	"Shirley's Curlies" people called it. It was always packed out.
HEIDI	We never came.

BEX	Did hundreds of shampoos and sets.
HEIDI	My Auntie Sheila did mine in their back room.
BEX	I used to sit in the back room here and do them magic painting books.
HEIDI	They were crap them! They went all soggy and fell to bits.
BEX	Oh I loved them, I thought they were magic.
HEIDI	She ruined my hair you know, my Auntie Sheila. All them cheap dyes and perms that burnt your head.
BEX	My mum wouldn't close, you see. Not even through her chemotherapy.
HEIDI	They can't have been good for you them dyes, you know?
BEX	No, that's right!
HEIDI	Once my hair fell out.
BEX	Yes, so did my mum's. But she still came to work. It was her life. Which wasn't always a good thing. Not for me anyway. Or for her, come to think of it
HEIDI	Got you through college though.
BEX	In fact it's probably what killed her.
HEIDI	I'll just go over this back bit again.
BEX	No leave it.
HEIDI	It's sticking out.
BEX	Leave it. You can't do it properly.
HEIDI	Hey up, you cheeky get!

BEX   Max hates it like this anyway, he thinks it looks
             common.

HEIDI   Common? It'll be like mine.

BEX   I'll go and get into my dress.

HEIDI   Can I ring Gary now then? Tell him to fetch
             me?

BEX   Fetch you what?

HEIDI   You know what I mean.

BEX   Collect you?

HEIDI   (*icy*) Whatever!

BEX   (*not apologising*) I'm only saying!

             (BEX *exits to storeroom.* HEIDI *rings Gary on
             her mobile.*)

HEIDI   It's me . . . What do you mean who? Me for
             chuff's sake. How many other women are
             ringing you up? . . . No I haven't, not yet . . .
             we can't book it yet, can we? Anyway come
             and pick me up . . . End of what? . . . Stuff the
             Simpsons, I need to get home and get changed
             or how am I gonna be part of the surprise . . . I
             know she knows anyway, but Max doesn't
             know that she knows so he's gonna wonder
             where I am . . . It's a disco and a free bar so we
             might as well go and get pissed up . . . No it
             won't be just wine, there'll be everything . . .
             I'll see you in five minutes, pip your horn
             twice.

             (BEX *enters from the storeroom. She is wearing
             a dress that is slightly too young for her and
             quite clinging.*)

HEIDI   Bloody hell!

BEX	What?
HEIDI	Well, it's different.
BEX	What do you mean?
HEIDI	Different to what you normally wear.
BEX	You mean that it doesn't suit me?
HEIDI	Well . . .
BEX	Because I know. It looks shit.
HEIDI	It doesn't look shit, it . . .
BEX	I should never have bought it. I knew when I tried it on.
HEIDI	I need to get used to it that's all.
BEX	But I thought; no, I'm boring I always go for the same old thing; a bloody trouser suit . . . I need to go sexy . . .
HEIDI	Right.
BEX	Convinced myself it was what I needed, or rather the assistant did.
HEIDI	That's their job. They're arseholes.
BEX	She said it was flattering. It's about as flattering as a sleeping bag, isn't it?
HEIDI	I wouldn't go that far.
BEX	She said it took years off me.
HEIDI	Mind you, that's what we do in here.
BEX	I didn't realise that I'd put on so much weight. I can't stop eating.

HEIDI	You've only put on about a stone though, haven't you?
BEX	A stone? I haven't put on a stone. I've put on about half a stone. Do I look like I've put on a stone?
HEIDI	You can get rid of a stone in a week.
BEX	By cutting your head off, yes I know!
HEIDI	On Atkins you can get rid of a stone in a week.
BEX	I can't go to the party like this.
HEIDI	Who's bothered?
BEX	I look worse than I've ever done in my life.
HEIDI	You don't
BEX	How do you know?
HEIDI	All right then, you do.
BEX	Oh shut up, you!
HEIDI	But I'll tell you sommat there's a lot of people look worse than you.
BEX	That's the trouble though, isn't it?
HEIDI	Eh?
BEX	That's how I've got like this; by constantly telling myself that I'm not that bad. I mean I don't need my arms waxing and I'm not Mrs Whitham!
HEIDI	I'll tell you sommat; Mrs Whitham never seems unhappy though, does she?
BEX	She's covering up you silly b . . . !

HEIDI	I don't think being unhappy is owt to do with being fat though, you know!
BEX	I didn't say that I was unhappy.
HEIDI	Well what are you then?
BEX	I'm just fed up; I've got lines around my eyes, saggy tits, grey hair . . .
HEIDI	Hey I've got a beard!
BEX	You can cut that off!
HEIDI	It's called getting older.
BEX	Yeh, well I don't want it.
HEIDI	You're giving into it. You're letting yourssen go, you don't care.
BEX	'Course I care, you silly bitch.
HEIDI	Well I go swimming and that, I try and dress up, and I don't eat chocolate, you know . . . I mean I have the odd cig but there's no calories is there? You're in a bubble, you're in what's called your "comfort zone."
BEX	And what are you – perfect?
HEIDI	Well I'll tell you what, I like a laugh, which is more than I can say for you.
BEX	(*becoming agitated*) Hey, hey, hey, I like a laugh.
HEIDI	When?
	(BEX *is becoming angry and emotional through the scene to the end of act one.*)
BEX	I like a laugh!

HEIDI	When?
BEX	I like a laugh!
HEIDI	You haven't laughed for ages!
BEX	(*stoic*) I like a laugh!
HEIDI	If you laughed you'd shit yourssen.
BEX	I like a laugh!
HEIDI	Well laugh at being overweight then!
BEX	I can't, can I? Because I hate myself for not going to the gym, for not counting points on my biscuits and for pigging out at every meal, that's why I hate my-bloody-self!
HEIDI	It's because nothing will happen if you don't, that's why you hate yourself!
BEX	Well nothing'll happen if you do, so what's the difference?
HEIDI	Well I don't want to be on my own, do I? I'm still on the market! You're not on the market you're off the market, aren't you?
BEX	Sometimes I wish I was on the bloody market to be honest!
HEIDI	I don't think you would!
BEX	Yeh well, I'll tell you something, shall I? Max was going to a "do" last week; and told me he didn't want me to go, said it wasn't my sort of thing. And do you know why; because he's ashamed of me, because all the other women are like footballer's wives or something and he's ashamed of me, and that's why I may end up on the market!
HEIDI	(*trying to quell this*) Well . . .

BEX	And when I say, "Do you think I've put weight on?" he says "Yeh you have". I mean why doesn't he lie to me? If he loved me he'd lie to me, wouldn't he?
HEIDI	Well . . .
BEX	That'd make me feel good, then maybe I'd want to loose some bloody weight.
HEIDI	No you wouldn't because if he said you weren't fat you wouldn't feel fat, so you'd think that you didn't need to lose any weight. Then you'd end up eating more because you felt good about him liking you and you wouldn't know that he thought you were fat, would you?
BEX	(*exhausted*) Oh I can't follow that!
HEIDI	And if he doesn't love you, why is he doing a party for you anyway?
BEX	It's not for me is it? It's for him! So he can show off! He's booked a swing band and he knows I like discos.
HEIDI	(*disapproving*) Oh is it a swing band, I thought it was a disco?
BEX	So did I, and it's my party!
HEIDI	Gary hates swing! He thought it was a disco!
BEX	And he's ordered dressed crab, which I absolutely hate, and ten thousand bloody vol-au-vents, which I'll obviously stuff myself with rather than talking to his mother the Queen!
HEIDI	Do you think there'll be curried baked beans then?
BEX	No, you're wrong, if you think he's doing it for me! It's like that hot tub, he's pretending that's

for me. It's for him, so he can say that he's got one at the golf club. Why would I want a hot tub? So that I can stagger over the side of it in the moonlight with my cellulite bobbling about? Oh yes that'd be good!

HEIDI   (*trying to help*) Well once you'd got in you'd be all right . . .

BEX   (*angst*) He never asks me what I want. Never! He just takes me for granted.

(*A horn is heard off stage. It is Gary.*)

HEIDI   I think that's Gary.

BEX   I do everything in the house!

(*A horn is heard off stage.*)

HEIDI   Yes that's Gary's! I said to pip twice.

BEX   I do absolutely everything and he wonders why I'm knackered.

HEIDI   (*preparing to exit*) Listen I'd better go, I'll see you there. You'll enjoy it when you get there you know it'll be a big surprise, you're just a bit emotional what with being forty and fat and all that! You'll love it when you get there won't you?

(HEIDI *exits grabbing her coat as she leaves.*)

See you later!

(BEX *is alone on stage. She eats a biscuit.*)

BEX   I can't frigging well wait!

(*Music. Blackout.*)

End of Act One.

ACT TWO

Scene One

The salon. The following morning. There is a similar atmosphere to the top of the play. The radio plays, BEX *is blow-drying a different* CLIENT'S *hair. (Again this is a stage-management role, using a different wig). She gives no indication of what happened last night, and is as effusive as ever.*

BEX   Well if you want pink, go for it. You've nothing to lose. I can't do it today though, but if you come back at the end of next week.

(*The phone rings.* BEX *tries to get it whilst blow drying the* CLIENT'S *hair, she extends the hairdryer's flex to its extreme. But she still finds it difficult to actually answer the phone. With the hairdryer blowing, the radio playing and the phone ringing. "I Want That Hair" is a vortex of confusion. After stretching as far as she can* BEX *eventually answers the phone.*)

"I Want That Hair!" No, no, sorry, you want "Hairsperience", there's a digit's difference. Okay. No problem. No it was no trouble at all, thanks for your call!

(BEX *returns the phone and makes her way back to the* CLIENT *with a slight difficulty, but then she picks up exactly where she left off.*)

I was pink once you know, 1981, I loved it! Everybody smiles at you when you've got pink hair. Mind you there's no wonder is there? Maybe I should go pink again? I fancy a bit of a change myself to be honest, and pink might just do it! Pink hair, a pair of stacked gothic boots and a long leather coat, that'd be a change, wouldn't it?

(*The phone rings once more.* BEX *once again goes through the torment of trying to answer*

the phone whilst continuing to dry the
CLIENT'S *hair. She eventually reaches the*
phone.)

"I Want That Hair!" No this is "I Want That
Hair". No I'm not a pet shop! Well have you
tried "Give The Dog A Bone?" Okay, thanks for
your call!

(BEX *returns the phone and goes back to*
drying her CLIENT'S *hair.*)

(*partly to herself*) Do we sell dog coats?

(BEX *is now back with her* CLIENT.)

No, if I was you, I wouldn't go all pink, not a
full colour, I'd go for streaks and do it through
the cap.

(BEX *burns the* CLIENT'S *head.*)

Sorry was that your ear?

(BEX *pulls the hairdryer away.*)

Anyway, to make it work properly you need to
blend it, so what you want is a deep pink
probably mixed with a seventy-seven, forty-
four. It'll look warm then and not too much in
your face. Unless you want it in your face that
is. Not literally in your face, on your head
obviously, but over your face, seventies kind
of thing, Phil Oakey. I loved the Human
League, did you? I mean a change might be
good for you really when you think about it!
That's what most people want when they come
in here. They come through that door, they
show me a photo and they say Bex, "I want
that hair." And I think you must be joking!
They've got some picture from *Hello* or *Cosmo*
and they say that's what I want; make me look
like Nicole Kidman, or Jordan and I think, "I'm
a blinking hairdresser not a plastic surgeon!"

They change their hair and think they've
changed their whole life. Then they start doing
things that any decent woman should never do
over thirty six; they start wearing halter neck
tops, bright red lipstick and they tuck their
jeans in their boots. I mean talk about saddos.

(BEX *is consumed in her philosophy*.)

No you don't come in here to change your hair
do you, you come in here to change your life!

(BEX *has finished the hair and stops the
drying. She rearranges the* CLIENT'S *hair*.)

Oh that's gone well today, hasn't it? How do
you feel about that?

(*Music. Blackout.*)

Scene Two

Two hours later. BEX *is alone in the salon. The radio plays
and she is putting away various bits of kit. She takes a moment
and looks at herself in the mirror, she is stoic, but something
isn't right. Enter* HEIDI, *slowly. She stumbles in looking rough.
She is wearing jeans tucked into her boots, and under a jacket
she wears a halter-neck top over a brightly coloured bra. You
can see her thong above the waist of her jeans. Silence.*

HEIDI   Oh!

BEX   Yes?

HEIDI   Oh hell!

BEX   What?

HEIDI   Oph.

BEX   Yes, well?

HEIDI   Friggin' hell I'm not good!

BEX	No?
HEIDI	Not good at all. My mouth, oh hell!
BEX	What about it?
HEIDI	Tastes like the bottom of a hamster cage.
BEX	How would you know?
HEIDI	Well . . . ?
BEX	Don't answer that!

(*A beat.*)

HEIDI	Sorry Bex!

(HEIDI *hangs up her jacket.*)

BEX	We open at nine, you know. Lisa 'My Dad's Won the Lottery' came in for her blow dry at ten past.
HEIDI	Oh shit.
BEX	And she can afford to go anywhere!
HEIDI	Lisa 'My Dad's Won the Lottery'?
BEX	Ten past nine!
HEIDI	She tips well and all!
BEX	Does she?
HEIDI	Usually.
BEX	She never tips me!

(*A beat.*)

Anyway she can afford to, can't she?

HEIDI	(*feeling ill*) Oh I feel like . . .
BEX	She waited half an hour but then she had some shopping to do.
HEIDI	Probably went to buy her lottery ticket, she always does on a Saturday! All that money and she still does five lines at 'weekend!
BEX	So that's cost me twenty-seven pounds fifty.
HEIDI	I had to get the bus!
BEX	So what's happened to Gary?
HEIDI	Oh he's plumbing for his ex-wife.
BEX	Well that's broad-minded of you!
HEIDI	Have you been on a bus lately? If you're not sick when you get on, you are by the time you get off.
BEX	Get a coffee.
HEIDI	(*moving gingerly*) I can't move my head.
BEX	You don't need to move your head do you? It's your arms you need to move.
	(*The phone rings.* BEX *looks at* HEIDI *who is making no attempt to answer it, though she winces at the noise it makes. Eventually* BEX *answers the phone, as* HEIDI *exits.*)
BEX	"I Want That Hair!" No, "Hairsperience" is the new one across the road. It's 634 it ends on, and this is 635 . . . No this is 635 . . . A Lime, Basil and Mandarin what? Oh a facial? No we don't do them, we just do hair! That's why we're called "I Want That Hair", and not "I Want That All Over Body Scrub!" And listen if you want the other place, put your glasses on and look the number up. Anyway thanks for your call, this is a recorded message and

you've been talking to Rebecca, for customer
services press one, for anything else shove
your handset right up your bum hole!

(BEX *ends the call. Music. Blackout.*)

Scene Three

Twenty minutes later. HEIDI *is off stage in the storeroom.* BEX
is upstage and is looking at the bookings book. She calls off to
HEIDI.

BEX   (*calls off*) Apparently Mrs Hilton can't come in
               today because the wheelchair man's off with
               flu, and her son's in Llandudno at a brass band
               concert and his wife's been disqualified from
               driving. (*To herself.*) Why she felt she wanted
               to tell me all that is anybody's guess but . . . !

               (HEIDI *enters from storeroom. She is still
               feeling rather unwell.*)

HEIDI   (*fiddling*) I'll tell you sommat, this thong is
               killing me. It was all right last night, but under
               these jeans it's no good.

BEX   You've got the same one on?

HEIDI   I slept in it!

BEX   (*distasteful*) Urgh!

HEIDI   I think I had a shower in it this morning to be
               honest, I can't remember. I was all over the
               place.

BEX   (*distasteful*) Urgh hell!

HEIDI   I'd forgot I'd got it on!

BEX   Spare me the detail, I feel a bit delicate as it is.

HEIDI   I've put the kettle on by the way!

BEX   You've managed to do something then?

    (HEIDI *stands and pontificates.*)

HEIDI   The thing is with a thong, when you're dancing your arse starts to eat it, doesn't it?

BEX   (*unhappy*) I really wouldn't know I've never worn one! I'm a big "hold-you-in" knicker woman!

HEIDI   Well I'm only telling you the truth.

BEX   Well we don't always want to hear the truth, darling!

HEIDI   You feel like it's gone a bit too far, don't you?

    (BEX *is still looking through the appointments book.*)

BEX   I'm not listening to you!

HEIDI   (*fiddling*) I'll go make that coffee and unhook it, shall I? I think it'll be much better if I can get it to rest across my cheek.

BEX   (*reading*) Oh please!

HEIDI   Mind you it's that tight it'll probably leave a ridge on my arse!

BEX   I'll get the coffee myself.

HEIDI   Don't worry, I'm going to wash my hands.

    (*The phone rings again.* HEIDI *answers it.*)

HEIDI   Hello . . . Oh not you again . . . (*To* BEX.) Change your phone people . . . Was it you yesterday? Or was it your mate? 'Cos whoever it was, the message is not getting through. Well how many of you are there? . . . How many? Well you're gonna get through some

money if they're all gonna give us a call.
What? . . . (*To* BEX.) He says he might ring me
anyway. (*To phone.*) Why is that then? (*To*
BEX.) He says he likes the sound of my voice.

BEX   (*reading upstage*) Is he deaf?

HEIDI   (*to the phone*) Are you deaf?

BEX   (*to herself*) You just can't get the staff!

HEIDI   (*to the phone*) Deaf! Are you deaf? Oh very
            funny. So what's your name? Callum? That's
            Irish, isn't it? No, I never noticed. I thought
            you were an Indian.

BEX   (*looking up*) Leave him alone, he won't know
            what he is talking to you!

            (*Still occupied, looking at* HEIDI.)

            Will you come off that phone?

HEIDI   So are you in Ireland now then? . . .
            Newcastle? Oh, that's not far from us, is it? I
            went up there once to see Culture Club.

BEX   (*astonished*) Culture Club? Bloody hell, how
            long ago was that?

            (HEIDI *responds to* BEX.)

HEIDI   I was only young!

BEX   (*not a fan*) Culture Club now!

            (HEIDI *is back on the phone.*)

HEIDI   Oh no, don't go yet . . . Oh does she? Does
            she work there as well? (*To* BEX.) His
            girlfriend's wanting him. (*To phone.*) Oh right
            then! (*To* BEX.) They're gonna go outside for a
            cig.

BEX   (*disbelieving*) How riveting!

HEIDI   (*to phone*) Well I'll tell you sommat, if you've
         got a girlfriend you shouldn't be leading
         people on . . . Oh come off it 'course you have
         . . . Friendly? It was more than friendly, it
         was suggestive . . . yes it was!

BEX   (*pleading*) He only said you had a nice voice.

HEIDI   In fact, who's your supervisor? I want to talk
         to him . . . !

BEX   (*shouts*) Will you come off that bloody phone!

HEIDI   (*shouting down the phone*) Yes and the same
         to you, you Geordie bastard!

         (HEIDI *puts the handset down.* BEX *looks at
         her.*)

BEX   (*loudly*) I thought he was Irish?

HEIDI   I thought he was Indian at first!

BEX   (*angrily*) Will you just do something?

HEIDI   (*exiting with cigarettes*) Oh I'll have to go for
         a fag, my head's killing me!

         (*Music. Blackout.*)

Scene Four

An hour later. The radio plays. BEX *sits in one of the stylist's
chairs and swivels around as she listens to the music. As she
sits she uses her legs to pull herself over to a box of
chocolates. She savours a chocolate for some time. After a
while* HEIDI *enters from the outside door. She has a bottle of
wine with her. She stands holding it and looking at* BEX, *who
turns off the radio.*

BEX   I thought you'd had enough last night?

HEIDI	I've just found this on the back step.
BEX	That was quick then.
HEIDI	What?
BEX	Callum, sending it all the way from Newcastle. He must have done it while his girlfriend went for another cigarette!
HEIDI	No, it's from India.
BEX	I didn't know they did wine in India!
HEIDI	Not India, India! Our India! India "can I go and get a sandwich?" India.
BEX	India "can I go and get a sandwich India", and we never see her again?
HEIDI	She left it stood on little a note!
BEX	So where's the note then?
HEIDI	Oh I've binned that.
BEX	Why?
HEIDI	It was nowt, that.
BEX	You mean you couldn't drink it?
HEIDI	It was just a load of nowt!
BEX	What was it, a thank you card?
HEIDI	You'd think it was, wouldn't you?
BEX	Well who was it for, me or you?
HEIDI	It was for both of us, so I read it and binned it!
BEX	Well didn't you think I might want to read it since half of it was for me?

HEIDI   It would have only upset you if you'd've read
           it anyway so . . .

BEX   Why would it?

HEIDI   Because it would!

BEX   Why?

HEIDI   Because it would!

           (*A beat.*)

BEX   Oh . . . right then.

           (*A beat.*)

           Why, what did she say in it?

HEIDI   I can't tell you!

BEX   You can!

HEIDI   I can't! Because it'd only upset you!

BEX   Why? What did it say?

HEIDI   It said she was going away with her boyfriend,
           and she didn't want anyone to know where she
           was going, all right? Satisfied?

BEX   Well that's not going to upset me, is it? I was
           planing to tell college about her in any case, I
           was going to dump her!

HEIDI   And then it said, she didn't want to be fat and
           forty and stuck in a dead-end hairdressers like
           this so . . . She said she couldn't see a future
           in it!

           (*A beat.*)

BEX   Oh, right!

HEIDI	That's why I binned it!
BEX	I'm glad you did now!
HEIDI	(*demonstrating the wine*) I mean it's cheap stuff is this Cava, but it's the thought that counts, isn't it?
BEX	(*slightly off centre*) Oh aye, it's the thought that counts.

(HEIDI *takes the bottle of wine off stage as* BEX *helps herself to another chocolate.*)

Cheeky bitch!

HEIDI	I know!
BEX	No future in hairdressing?
HEIDI	(*exasperated*) I know!

(HEIDI *re-enters and makes her way over to the chocolates.*)

BEX	How did she know?
HEIDI	I know.
BEX	She was never here!

(HEIDI *sits and they both sit sharing the box of chocolates. They eat one after the other and savour them. This goes on for a while. When they speak their mouths are full.*)

Have you had one of these soft ones?

| HEIDI | What are they strawberry creams or sommat? |
| BEX | Do you suck them or do you bite straight into them? |

(*A beat.*)

HEIDI   Who me?

BEX   Well there's only you here isn't there? India's
                run off to India or somewhere.

                (*A beat.*)

HEIDI   I bite straight into them.

                (*A beat.*)

BEX   (*sucking*) I don't.

HEIDI   (*chewing*) Don't you?

BEX   (*sucking*) I suck them.

HEIDI   (*chewing*) I don't.

BEX   (*sucking*) Makes them last longer.

                (*A beat.*)

HEIDI   (*chomping and speaking at the same time*) I
                can't do that me, I'm a chomper!

BEX   (*sucking*) Are you?

HEIDI   I'm straight in, I like to fill my mouth.

BEX   (*sucking*) Too much for me that. Too much
                flavour all at once.

HEIDI   I like to know I've had them.

                (*A beat.*)

BEX   (*sucking*) I don't think I'd enjoy it as much, if
                I went straight in!

                (*A beat.*)

HEIDI   Why not?

BEX	They're gone too quick.
	(*A beat.*)
HEIDI	Yeh but they're all gone eventually aren't they, so what difference does it make as long as you've enjoyed them?
	(*A beat.*)
BEX	They're a waste of money really, aren't they?
HEIDI	They are really.
BEX	I'm mean all we do is eat them, then they're gone! A waste of money!
	(*A beat.*)
HEIDI	Well these weren't a waste of money because we didn't buy them, Mrs Whitham left 'em last week.
BEX	(*recalling*) Oh yes, she did.
HEIDI	I mean I think they're out of date, but . . .
BEX	It's the thought that counts.
HEIDI	Yes it is, yes!
BEX	(*easily*) It's the thought that counts.
	(*A beat.*)
HEIDI	How many have you had anyway?
BEX	About ten. How many have you had?
HEIDI	(*reluctant*) Fifteen!
BEX	Fifteen?
HEIDI	I had some while you were making the coffee!

BEX	Fifteen?
HEIDI	I don't eat chocolate usually, but . . .
BEX	Fifteen?
HEIDI	To be honest my stomach's a bit upset.
BEX	There's no wonder if you've had fifteen. I've only had ten.
HEIDI	Well ten's a lot.
BEX	It's not as many as fifteen!
	(HEIDI *stands, moves down stage and looks out towards the street.*)
HEIDI	Well I'm a bit stressed out!
BEX	There's no wonder you're stressed out if you've just had fifteen of these!
HEIDI	I think last night got to me! You know all the build up? I've still got a splitting headache.
BEX	I've probably put another six pounds on, that's how stressed out I am!
	(*A beat.*)
HEIDI	(*looking across the road*) Packed out over there if you look!
BEX	I don't want to look.
HEIDI	They're doing "two for one".
BEX	Two for one?
HEIDI	A manicure and a haircut, or a massage and a bum rub.
BEX	A bum rub?

HEIDI   You know, two for one!

BEX   Do they do a bum rub?

HEIDI   I think they do actually.

BEX   Oh no I wouldn't fancy that!

HEIDI   Mind you, you can't really do two for one at a
           hairdressers like this can you? Unless, you
           have it done, and then have it done again.

BEX   (*helping herself to another chocolate*) Yes
           that'd be novel! "Oh it's lovely that, will you
           wash it and do it again?"

HEIDI   Or you could take somebody with you I
           suppose – get a cut and then get your Grannie
           a perm.

BEX   (*sucking*) That's not a bad idea.

HEIDI   What's the difference between "two for one"
           and "buy one get one free" anyway?

BEX   (*sucking*) There isn't one!

HEIDI   So why do they have two ways of saying it? I
           mean "three for two", that's different; that's
           buy two, get one free, but that's not as good,
           because you've got a storage problem,
           especially if it's sommat big. I think "buy one,
           get one free" sounds best, sounds like you're
           getting more of a bargain, doesn't it? Because
           you're buying one and you're getting one free!

BEX   You do with two for one! You pay for one but
           you get an extra one free. (*To herself.*) Dear
           me!

HEIDI   (*noticing someone across the road*) Hey, I've
           just seen Carlene "what-they-call-her" go in
           there.

BEX	(*sucking*) Carlene what-they-call-her?
HEIDI	He must have won something at the Casino because she's with two Chinese women.
BEX	(*sucking*) Carlene what-they-call-her is going in there now!
HEIDI	I bet they're going there because they've got that Bombay Mix. Did you know that they'd got all that? They have it in little bowls, Bombay Mix and pine nuts.
BEX	(*sucking*) Do they?
HEIDI	You don't have owt like that, do you?
BEX	No, we don't have anything like that! That's because we're a hairdressers!
	(*A beat.*)
HEIDI	(*comes away from the window*) Hey, a good party, wasn't it?
BEX	Not bad!
HEIDI	That swing band weren't bad were they? And you like a dance don't you?
BEX	When I've had a drink!
HEIDI	What was it supposed to be?
BEX	(*sucking*) Dancing, that's what it was supposed to be. But you shouldn't do it over the age of thirty-nine! My back's killing me.
HEIDI	I know, I still feel a bit off it to be honest. I was all over the shop, did you see me?
BEX	(*dryly*) Oh yes, I saw you!
HEIDI	A good night though.

BEX	The hair of the dog! That's what we need.
HEIDI	You're not wrong there.
BEX	Well there's always that bottle from India.
HEIDI	Oh yes there's always that!
BEX	I mean it's cheap stuff but . . .
	(*A beat.*)
HEIDI	(*shyly*) Hey, shall I open it then?
BEX	(*sucking*) Well we're not exactly run off our feet are we, maybe if we had some pine nuts we would be but . . . ! Go on. If you open it, I'll have one glass!
HEIDI	Are you serious?
BEX	It's only a bottle of Cava, we're not going to go mad are we?
HEIDI	Hey you never know, let's keep the party going, eh?
BEX	(*dryly*) Oh yes, absolutely.
	(HEIDI *makes her way off stage, as she exits she calls to* BEX.)
HEIDI	(*calling*) Hey anyway, you know last night?
BEX	(*calling after her*) Yes, I was there. Go on . . .
HEIDI	(*calling*) Who was that fat lad with his shirt hanging out who was dancing?
BEX	(*calling*) That was my husband, darling!
HEIDI	(*calling*) No, I know him!

BEX   (*dryly*) They all looked like fat lads dancing to me! In fact I looked like a fat lass dancing.

(HEIDI *enters with an opened bottle of Cava and two mugs.*)

HEIDI   (*the Cava*) It didn't really go "pop" so I'm not sure how good it is!

BEX   Did it do anything?

HEIDI   Not really! (*The Cava.*) You can get this in Morrisons for four pounds, because Gary got us a box at Christmas, I mean it looks like Champagne but it's only sparkling wine really isn't it, they dress it up to make you feel good about drinking it!

BEX   It's as good as Champagne but they can't call it Champagne!

HEIDI   Why not?

BEX   Because it's not from Champagne.

HEIDI   This isn't from Champagne, it's from Morrisons I think, because Gary got us a box at Christmas.

BEX   (*philosophical*) Yes, nothing is what it appears any more!

HEIDI   And I think you can get it at Aldi. Oh no it's that Asti Spumanti you can get at Aldi, isn't it?

(HEIDI *offers* BEX *a mug of cava.*)

BEX   (*dryly*) Sod their pine nuts, look at us! A cuppa Cava and it's not even three o'clock! The shop is empty and we've only got a shampoo and set at a quarter to six but are we bothered?

HEIDI   Well . . . ?

BEX   Yes we are, but we're only having one so
               cheers anyway!

               (BEX *and* HEIDI *toast each other*.)

HEIDI   Cheers!

               (*They drink together*.)

BEX   Here's to us!

HEIDI   Happy birthday!

BEX   It was on Thursday actually, but . . . !

HEIDI   I thought it was last night?

BEX   (*easily*) Thursday, and I didn't get a card!

HEIDI   I gave you one last night though!

BEX   You didn't give me one on Thursday though!

HEIDI   I didn't know it was on Thursday, did I? That's
               why!

BEX   Anyway, it's the thought that counts.

               (*A beat*.)

HEIDI   (*sipping her drink*) Hey, why did all them
               blokes keep shouting "hooters" at me and
               Gary?

BEX   Because they're arseholes!

HEIDI   I thought they were shouting "shoot us".

BEX   (*dryly*) Wishful thinking that!

HEIDI   Gary nearly did. He had his doggin' gun in't
               car.

BEX	Do you know you can never find a good maniac with a gun when you need one!
HEIDI	I don't think they liked his ponytail to be honest!
BEX	(*thoughtful*) Well it didn't suit him when he let it down though, did it? He looked like Lemmy!
HEIDI	Who?
BEX	Lemmy from Motorhead!
HEIDI	Who the chuff!
BEX	Lemmy, Lemmy from Motorhead! I had a boyfriend from Barnsley who was into all their stuff! I was a Punk, and he was a Grebo, we should have been locked up. Just walking down the street we frightened people to death.

(HEIDI *sits in a stylist's chair.*)

HEIDI	I thought they were out of order to be honest. That's why Gary left.
BEX	(*dryly*) I thought you'd had a lovers tiff!
HEIDI	No, no they were getting on his tits.
BEX	They work with Max.
HEIDI	You were lucky he went home because otherwise he would have smacked somebody.
BEX	He should have smacked Max's mother!
HEIDI	They didn't give a chuff about your birthday though, did they? I mean they might have designer gear but . . . I mean how many of your proper mates were there anyway?
BEX	Well, there was Sandra.

HEIDI   Oh I met her, she's a *Star Wars* Trekkie isn't
           she?

BEX   Her mum and dad knew Mr Sulu.

HEIDI   Really?

BEX   He's stayed at their house.

HEIDI   Who's Mr Sulu then?

BEX   Mr Sulu?

HEIDI   Yes who's that then?

BEX   He's in *Star Trek*.

HEIDI   What, Mr Sulu out of *Star Trek*?

BEX   Yes, that Mr Sulu!

HEIDI   What, "Beam me up Scotty", *Star Trek* Mr
           Sulu?

BEX   Yes, yes bloody *Star Trek*, there's only one!

HEIDI   Well how the chuff did you end up with friends
           in *Star Trek* and you're doing this?

BEX   Her mam was friends with my mam. She's had a
           bad time, her husband ran off to Australia.

HEIDI   Maybe she beamed him up?

BEX   She'd have to have beamed him down.

HEIDI   Where were your friends from university
           though?

BEX   Max asked them but they said that it was too
           short notice.

HEIDI   Hey? I'd known about it for three months!

BEX   I think Max's moved on anyway.

HEIDI   What, to a set of tossers?

BEX   Well he's a bit like that at times, but . . .

HEIDI   Well how come you didn't notice that when
          you first met him then?

BEX   Hey?

HEIDI   That he's a bit of a tosser!

BEX   I don't know. I think I felt sorry for him.

HEIDI   Felt sorry for him?

BEX   Well when I was at University, there was this
          group of us all training to be teachers; we had
          a right laugh . . .

HEIDI   Oh yeh?

BEX   Hey, hey, we had a right laugh.

HEIDI   All right, I believe you!

BEX   No you don't!

HEIDI   Was Max a teacher then?

BEX   No! He was a chemistry student. That's the
          thing; the education students had all the best
          parties. Do you remember Hot Gossip?

HEIDI   (*drinking*) Hot Gossip? Chuffing hell, how old
          are we? 'Course I do, they're all grannies now
          you know? I think two of 'em are dead!

BEX   Well we had a group called Loose Elastic! We
          danced at the college balls.

HEIDI   What, and your knickers kept coming down?

BEX	Eh?
HEIDI	(*explaining her joke*) Did your knickers keep coming down?
BEX	(*as a fact*) No!
HEIDI	I just thought, you know; with the name.
BEX	(*enjoying the memory*) And we had this kidnap squad; a couple of my English group and some of the big PE lads. If somebody was getting on your nerves you could contact us, and we'd abduct them from the campus, tie them up, blindfold them and drive them off in Barry Winterbottom's car. Then we'd leave them in the middle of nowhere.
HEIDI	Gary nearly got sent down for doing that you know!
BEX	We got more than one call to kidnap Max. He'd gone off with somebody's girlfriend I think it was, he was so full of himself. Anyway we dumped him on the edge of Carlton Woods, but he was upset because his mum and dad were coming and he couldn't get back.
HEIDI	They were bringing him his curried baked beans.
BEX	Anyway I went back for him on my moped.
HEIDI	You had a moped?
BEX	A little purple one!
HEIDI	Chuff me! Pink hair, a purple moped, what were you on?
BEX	I fancied him; everybody in my group did.
HEIDI	He's small though isn't he? I hadn't really noticed until he was talking to Gary!

BEX	Yes but Gary's a giant, isn't he?
HEIDI	I've always gone for big men.
BEX	I mean Gary's a giant!
HEIDI	There's sommat to get hold of, do you know what I mean?
BEX	How tall is he?
HEIDI	I mean with little men it's like they're not finished, isn't it?
BEX	Anyway, there was something about Max. He was very confident. When his mum and dad had gone he came round to my room with a bottle of Ljutomer Riesling, to thank me for bringing him back and he realised we were from the same area. He didn't know it at the time but he was the first.
HEIDI	You're joking?
BEX	No!
HEIDI	So there's only been him?
BEX	Well that would be telling.
HEIDI	(*excitedly*) So there's been others?
	(*A beat.*)
BEX	(*sadly*) No, there's only been him.
HEIDI	So how do you know if he's any good?
BEX	Well I suppose I don't really, do I?
HEIDI	Because I thought Wayne was good until I met Grant, but I thought Grant was clumsy when I met Gino. And Gino was rubbish compared to Craig, I mean I loved him, but Craig was shit

compared to Hanif, and Hanif was an amateur compared to Gary.

BEX   Well to be honest the week before I'd been on a CND rally in London and I was that worried that the world was going to end, that I was on a bit of a mission.

HEIDI   Oh hell!

BEX   Twenty-two years later!

HEIDI   When I was at tech I didn't have any of that. I had to get the bus straight home and pick up our Dean from my mam's. I mean I didn't really have a bloke for about three years really.

BEX   Sounds like you've made up for it since though, doesn't it?

HEIDI   I deserve it an' all.

BEX   I wish more of my Uni friends could have come really, although Max wasn't really a part of them.

HEIDI   That's why he didn't invite them. He might have been scared they'd kidnap him again.

BEX   (easily) That would have been good, him and his mother.

HEIDI   Why do you think you've lasted so long?

BEX   I don't know to be honest; I mean we've had some good times you know. But now it's just what we are; it's too difficult to contemplate change.

             (HEIDI knocks back her drink. She moves to look outside the salon.)

HEIDI   Anyway you did a nice speech. Thanking him and his mam and that.

BEX	Oh!
HEIDI	What?
BEX	You're joking aren't you?
HEIDI	No I thought you did it well. I couldn't stand up and talk like that!
BEX	It was a load of rubbish.
HEIDI	(*softly*) I thought it was real nice.
BEX	I only said what was expected of me. I mean Max would have had a coronary if I'd've told him what I really thought about it.
HEIDI	How do you mean?
BEX	Well you know said what I really felt, for once!
HEIDI	I always say what I think, me!
BEX	(*acting it*) "Thank you darling for organising a lousy party, that I didn't want in the first place. For getting a swing band when I'd have preferred a disco and for getting your mother to make a thousand mushroom vol-au-vents when I'm trying to lose weight."
HEIDI	Oh I thought the band was good, especially that bloke on the sax.
BEX	He must have been ninety-four!
HEIDI	He could swing his hips though.
BEX	They probably weren't his to swing. In fact we were lucky they didn't fall off. No, I should have told the truth for once, but I never do. I'm just so bloody accepting!

HEIDI   Well you are, yeh, really.

BEX   And they were all his stupid mates jumping
                 about . . .

HEIDI   And in the Conservative Club and all?

BEX   No common sense, any of them . . .

HEIDI   (*effusive*) I mean I'd have to say it me. I have
                 to let it out. If you don't, it eats away at you.

BEX   I should have stood up and told him I'd had
                 enough.

HEIDI   (*as a fact*) It eats away at you if you don't.

                 (BEX *helps herself to another glass of Cava
                 through the speech.*)

BEX   Because you know when I think about it what
                 have I actually done over the years for me?

HEIDI   Well . . .

BEX   Holidays I didn't want to go on, that I always
                 have to book. Dinners I didn't want to cook.
                 Hours spent at Tumble Tots and God knows
                 what, which was great, but there were some
                 weeks when I just . . . And all so he could get
                 on his feet. You know he thinks that this is not
                 a proper job.

HEIDI   No?

BEX   He thinks this is a joke!

HEIDI   It's your life though isn't it?

BEX   Always putting me down.

HEIDI   I mean you've put your life into it, haven't
                 you?

BEX   He thinks I'm doomed in here, told me as much
           last night.

HEIDI   (*mock shock*) He never!

BEX   (*worse still*) He even told me to tone it down
           when I was dancing with our Rachael.

HEIDI   Hey, she's a good dancer, isn't she?

BEX   And like a moron I did! At my own fortieth!

           (BEX *downs another drink*.)

HEIDI   Was it jive?

BEX   You know she's got gold medals?

HEIDI   She never!

BEX   She has.

HEIDI   For jiving?

BEX   Gold medals.

HEIDI   I thought she looked good.

BEX   And it was me that took her to that.

HEIDI   You must be proud of her? In fact it looked
           like you'd picked a bit of it up yourself!

           (BEX *is trying the bottle but it is empty.*)

BEX   Hey, I'm only gold tap!

HEIDI   You never are?

BEX   I'm gold tap.

HEIDI   You're not!

BEX   I'm bloody gold tap!

HEIDI   And you're forty and all.

BEX   I can't do it now but . . .

HEIDI   Gold taps, eh?

BEX   (*sarcastic*) Oh aye, gold taps on everything.
           And I toned it down when he asked me! I
           wonder why I stay sometimes. Twenty-two
           years . . .

HEIDI   I mean I've left four after three years. And
           with one I only stayed nine months. And with
           some I've done a couple of weeks.

BEX   I can't though. I just accept?

HEIDI   You should do more of what you want.

BEX   But I'm not Shirley Valentine though, am I?

HEIDI   No you're not, no.

BEX   I'm not Shirley Valentine. I mean I wish I
           was!

HEIDI   Well you could be!

BEX   Sat on a Greek beach with a glass of Ouzo . . .

HEIDI   It's easy these days.

BEX   And little bit of calamari!

HEIDI   I know somebody who's done it!

BEX   Shirley Valentine, wouldn't that be nice?

HEIDI   Well change then, you can do!

BEX   Eh?

HEIDI   Change your name, Elvis Macdonald did, he
           used to be called Keith; he changed his name.

BEX   I was on about the film . . .

HEIDI   Oh right.

BEX   Where she runs off.

HEIDI   Oh right! I'm always running off me!

BEX   She ran away to Greece.

HEIDI   I ran away to Gilberdyke once from school.

BEX   And if I did, I'm not sure anyone would be
         actually bothered.

HEIDI   Oh they would.

BEX   Who?

HEIDI   Oh they would!

BEX   Who?

HEIDI   Well . . .

BEX   Who though?

HEIDI   Well your Rachael would, wouldn't she?

BEX   You wouldn't though, would you?

HEIDI   Oh I would . . .

         (BEX *holds the bottle.*)

BEX   Hey, shall we have another?

HEIDI   Another, we've already had a bottle!

BEX   Listen I've got another two in the back.
         Chardonnay! The Rep left them.

HEIDI	Chardonnay? The Rep? And do you know what? I've been calling her Melanie for the last two years!
BEX	Oh, that's funny.
HEIDI	Is it?
BEX	You know, you're great company, you are!
HEIDI	Am I?
BEX	Yes you are!
HEIDI	Am I, honest?
BEX	Yes!
HEIDI	Oh thanks, I didn't know!
BEX	I don't know what I'd do without you!
HEIDI	Oh, isn't that nice!

(HEIDI *laughs insanely.* BEX *cackles at her.*)

(*Music. Blackout.*)

Scene Five

Later. The radio plays. BEX *is looking through the bookings book. She is on the phone. She is clearly under the influence and is giving a client a hard time.*

| BEX | Well when can you come? I can't hear you? Shall I come to you? No I'm serious, I'll do a home visit Like my mother used to . . . I'll tell you what, why don't you ring 625634? It's "Hairsperience". Do you want that "Hairsperience"? They'll be able to do you a wash, blow dry perm and fold your legs into a drawer for ninety quid . . . I am being serious! No this is Rebecca . . . Listen, would you like to |

ring tomorrow when we're not as busy? 'Cos
I'm a bit busy at the minute, okay? Thanks!

(BEX *puts down the phone but it's a bit of a
problem.* HEIDI *enters with another drink.*)

Oh hell, I'm all over the shop.

HEIDI   (*edgy*) I'm back to last night, I am!

BEX   Oh aye, Belle of the Ball you were in that dress!
           No wonder they were shouting at you!

HEIDI   Aye, well I know how to have a good time, I
           do!

BEX   I was only going to have one glass. I never do
           what I say I'm going to, that's my trouble. One
           day I will, one day I'll change. I promise
           myself that, one day I'll change.

HEIDI   You should just think, "sod it" and do sommat
           different!

BEX   It's not that easy though is it? Where would I
           go? What would I do? There's too much to
           worry about . . .

HEIDI   You and your chuffin' worrying.

           (BEX *becomes determined.*)

BEX   Okay, so let's say I leave Max and I'm on my
           own in a flat because we've had to split the
           house. I won't meet anyone else because I'm
           fat and forty you said that yourself, and I'd be
           working all the time, wouldn't I?

HEIDI   Yeh, but at least you'd be able to do what you
           wanted, and you wouldn't have him and his
           mother's curried baked beans to worry about,
           would you? You need to break out, you do.

BEX   I know.

HEIDI   You need a "makeover", you do.

BEX   I know that!

HEIDI   You need to start again!

BEX   (*unsure*) Oh I don't know about that!

HEIDI   Yes you do!

BEX   But how could I, if I was stuck with all this?

HEIDI   Yes you do!

BEX   Well I can't. It's not in my nature.

         (*She starts to become emotional.*)

         I'm a giver you see, like my Mother was
         I want to give to people, I want to please
         people!

HEIDI   Well you could always go back to teaching.

BEX   (*horrified*) Oh not now I couldn't. I'd worry
         that I might get knifed.

HEIDI   In primary school?

BEX   No you see I couldn't close this place no matter
         what happens, it meant too much to my Mum. I
         mean I gave to her you know, I nursed her, I
         mean I wanted to . . . And I wanted the best for
         Rachael; and Max's not really a bad husband I
         suppose, but he takes me for granted . . .

         (*She is getting even more emotional.*)

         I just wish that I got a bit more back . . .

HEIDI   Oh God.

BEX   (*through tears*) What?

HEIDI	(*harder*) You're pathetic, you know that don't you? Pathetic!
BEX	Oh don't say that.
HEIDI	You never stop once you've started, do you?
BEX	(*appealing*) Do you think it's menopausal?
HEIDI	No I think it's feeling sorry for yourself, that's what I think!
BEX	(*upset*) I'm so lonely. So lonely Heidi, and nobody knows! Nobody knows how lonely it gets!
HEIDI	(*harder*) Yeh they do!
BEX	I mean you haven't lost your Mum have you? You can pick up the phone and she's there. I saw Gloria last night trying to dance with my dad and I thought why's she here, silly fat cow! Why is she here?
	(*A beat.*)
HEIDI	(*ice*) That never changes love! That never goes away.
BEX	What do you mean?
	(*Silence.*)
HEIDI	It's twelve years, four months and three days since I lost our Dean! It never goes away.
	(*A beat.*)
BEX	Oh I'm . . .
HEIDI	(*becomes emotional*) He got beat up in town. He'd had these dreadlocks done; wanted to be like his Dad, always had to be different.

BEX   I'm . . .

HEIDI   He was only fourteen, I mean I know he
           shouldn't have been out drinking but what can
           you do with 'em at that age?

BEX   I know.

HEIDI   They hit him that hard he never woke up. I sat
           by his bed for six days.

BEX   I had no idea!

HEIDI   You've got to move on, Becky. Not just for
           you, but for them. You've just got to live, just
           get on with it or get out. Your Mam wouldn't
           want to hear you talk like that, would she?

BEX   (*tearful*) But the thing is, if I closed the shop
           you'd have no job, would you? I mean I
           couldn't do that to you. I couldn't do that to
           you. Because we're a team, aren't we? We're a
           team. And we'll beat anybody we will!
           "Hairsperience"! Mark Hill! Me and you'll
           beat anybody, won't we?

           (*A beat.*)

HEIDI   Well, we would but . . .

BEX   But what?

HEIDI   Well . . . I think I'm going.

BEX   Eh?

HEIDI   I think I'm going to go!

           (*A beat.*)

BEX   Where to?

HEIDI   I've been offered another job.

BEX	A hairdressing job?
HEIDI	Yes you cheeky cow, a hairdressing job!
BEX	But we're a team, aren't we?
HEIDI	It's what I've always done. I did it at "Mr Snips", and "Imij", and even did at Phillip Sheridan's, and "British Hairwaves".
BEX	Oh right!
HEIDI	I have to move on, I can't let the grass grow.
BEX	So where are you going then?
	(*Silence.*)
HEIDI	(*carefully*) I'm er . . . I'm going across the road.
	(*Silence.*)
BEX	What, to . . . ?
HEIDI	He's offered me a stylist's job . . . I mean . . .
BEX	After all you've said?
HEIDI	It's not personal. I can still come for a coffee and that.
BEX	(*disbelieving*) I don't . . .
HEIDI	It's just that I can't stay in one place. I mean I bet I won't be there two minutes; and then I'll be off again. I mean I haven't told 'em that but . . .
BEX	You just don't give a shit about me, do you? I thought we were a team?
HEIDI	Well let's be honest you don't really give a shit about *me*, do you? It's all a charade!

BEX	Oh a charade is it?
HEIDI	Well in the four years I've been here you've never even asked me out for a drink once.
BEX	What about Christmas?
HEIDI	Christmas doesn't count.
BEX	(*exasperated*) Well, I've never been out for a drink, I'm always rushing to get home.
HEIDI	Well I wasn't going to leave until the end of the month anyway so . . .
BEX	Oh yeh, make sure you get your wages.
HEIDI	Actually I think there might be some holiday pay an' all.
BEX	Well you know what you can do with that don't you? Stick it up with your bloody thong.
HEIDI	(*trying to get it together*) I knew you'd get nasty and there's no need.
	(BEX *is frustrated and angry. She tries to manoeuvre herself around the salon but is a little too drunk to be effective.*)
BEX	You sit there, you drink my wine, you eat my chocolates, you read half my letter; you drink like a fish at my party and then you're off.
HEIDI	It's not like that, I have to do it for me, that's what I'm like. It's not personal!
BEX	(*angrily*) It bloody well is personal though, you know! Well I'll tell you something, go then, go, I'll show you, you'll soon wish that you'd stayed here.
HEIDI	No I won't, not if you're going to be like that!

BEX   Oh yes you will.

HEIDI   (*angry*) You're going to make me say stuff I
               don't want to in a minute.

BEX   (*loudly*) Say it, say it! Come on, spit it out. If
               you've got something to say that you don't
               want to!

HEIDI   Listen, I was grateful for the job because it was
               my first after our Dean; apart from my mobile
               stuff.

BEX   But . . . ?

HEIDI   But be honest, this is not going anywhere, is
               it? I mean Carlos over there . . .

BEX   Oh it's Carlos now, that puff in a pink T-shirt
               with a pierced stomach. It's bloody Carlos
               now! How continental! Carlos? Good grief
               where do they get 'em from? He's probably
               from Scunthorpe or somewhere!

HEIDI   He's from Driffield actually but you know he
               trained with Mark Hill, don't you?

BEX   (*strongly*) I don't bloody care who he trained
               with!

HEIDI   He's opening all over. They reckon that I
               might even have to move to Howden.

BEX   (*mocking*) Howden?

HEIDI   I know!

BEX   (*loudly*) Hold the front page!

HEIDI   (*proudly*) Hey, its two buses!

BEX   You knew I wanted to change things in here.

HEIDI   But you'll never do it though, will you?

         (BEX *is aggressive.*)

BEX   Well you're wrong about that.

HEIDI   I hope I am.

BEX   (*determined*) You're going to be wrong about
         that.

HEIDI   I have to do what's best for me. And the thing
         is you're not properly trained, are you? It's not
         really a proper hairdresser's, is it?

BEX   How the hell did you work that out?

HEIDI   You didn't go to tech like me did you, you
         learned on the job. It's like me going to be a
         teacher. I couldn't do it as good as you
         because I haven't been properly trained!

BEX   What are you saying, that I'm not a good
         enough hairdresser now?

HEIDI   Well let's be honest, I'm not going to learn owt
         new from you, am I?

         (*Silence.*)

BEX   Well I'll tell you what. Here's something new.
         Get your coat, pack your bag and leave!

HEIDI   And now, you're being awful!

BEX   (*shouting*) Awful? I only took you on because
         I felt sorry for you! I mean look at the way you
         dress, you're embarrassing! And mucky? You
         can't even change your bloody thong!

HEIDI   That was a mistake, that!

BEX   And the shite you come out with, and your
         breath? I mean do me a favour! I'm glad

you're going because I've had enough of working with the bearded woman. Go on, get out!

HEIDI   Well I tell you something for nothing, your husband was all over me last night; he had his hand down me thong if you must know.

BEX   Well you're not the first so don't worry about it!

HEIDI   He was all over me!

BEX   Well why didn't you stop him?

HEIDI   How could I? I didn't want to offend you!

BEX   Just get out!

HEIDI   You know why I'm going don't you?

BEX   I'm not even interested!

HEIDI   Yeh, because you're jealous, because you're too scared to do the same. You're trapped! Well I don't want that!

BEX   Get!

            (*Silence.*)

HEIDI   I'll have to get Gary to call for me!

BEX   Out!

HEIDI   I can't go on the bus like this can I, I'll be as sick as a dog!

BEX   (*anxious*) I'm going to get some fresh air because I can't stand it in here! I can't stand all this upset! You've got to me you have, you've got to me! When I get back I want you to have gone, right, please, I want you bloody gone!

HEIDI   Oh I knew you'd be funny about it!

                 (BEX *grabs her coat and exits out of the main
                 salon door.* HEIDI *gets out her mobile phone.*)

HEIDI   It's me . . . Yeh I've told her . . . Well there's
                 time for us to go to Tenerife now, isn't there?
                 Oh you should've seen her. I mean she was
                 crying as it was . . . Hey I felt that bad I nearly
                 didn't tell her! Yes I know you hate swing
                 bands, and you thought they were all farts, I
                 said that, I told her that! I know, you could
                 have shot 'em and I'm proud that you didn't,
                 I'm proud that you decided to go home . . .
                 Well I couldn't, could I? It would have looked
                 rude . . . Hey listen, I was not egging him on!
                 Gary he was pissed up. Not as pissed up as
                 him. Well I am a bit, we opened a bottle so I
                 need you to come and get me. Hey, I am not
                 drunk up all the time. Look just be quick! She's
                 having a panic do! I'll be outside
                 "Hairsperience" . . . Ten minutes. Alright! I'm
                 not that pissed I can cross a chuffin' road!

                 (*She closes the phone and staggers around the
                 salon gathering her stuff together. As she exits
                 she takes with her the remainder of the box of
                 chocolates and a plant.*)

                 Oh hell!

                 (*Blackout. Music.*)

                             Scene Six

Six weeks later. BEX *is blow-drying a* CLIENT. *She now has
pink hair and wears more fashionable clothes.*

BEX   I thought, no, I'm not going to be part of the
                 wallpaper, I'm going to be different, because I
                 am different, but nobody knows I'm different,
                 because I don't look different. But now people

know I'm different; pink's a sign, it tells
people; she's different! You see you can
change yourself by changing your hair! I
thought you couldn't, but you can! What I've
done is change how people see me! I'm no
longer saying, dull and boring, I'm saying pink
and exciting, because deep down that's what I
used to be! Oh yes, everybody smiles at you
when you've got pink hair. And then you smile
back, which makes the world a better place. I
mean I'm smiling all the time now, I want
bloody locking up really. I mean it's not going
to change my life overnight but it's changed
how I feel and that's a first step . . . The next
step is to change the salon. I'm going for pale
greens, naturals. But you can't do it all at
once! The thing is Max is going to Dubai for
three months so Rachael and I are going to do
it. It's her design; I mean she knows what's in.
I mean it might not be perfect but we'll have a
laugh, because I like a laugh! (*Looking at the*
CLIENT'*s hair.*) Do you know it's gone ever so
nice at the back to say it's so short! You didn't
get a cup of tea, did you? (*Calling, off.*) India!
(*To* CLIENT.) She's been ever so good since she
came back. I think she missed the money! And
whatever you say, it is a skill for life. I mean I
wouldn't really want our Rachael doing it.
She's very clever you know and I think she's
got university in mind. Wants to be a
choreographer. Did you see her as Dandini?
And she's a lovely voice. I said to her, Rachael
if you ever get famous you can take me with
you, I'll do your hair!

(BEX *stops and look at the* CLIENT.)

So are you going away anywhere nice this
year?

(*Music plays as* BEX *continues. Fade to
blackout. Curtain.*)